MEN ARE FROM DETROIT

WOMEN ARE FROM PARIS

CARTOONS BY WOMEN
EDITED BY ROZ WARREN

THE CROSSING PRESS
FREEDOM, CA 95019

Library of Congress Cataloging-in-Publication Data
Men are from Detroit, women are from Paris : cartoons by women /
    edited by Roz Warren
        p.   cm.
    ISBN 0-89594-748-X
    1. Men--Caricatures and cartoons. 2. American wit and humor,
    Pictorial. I. Warren, Rosalind, 1954-
    NC1426.M375 1995
    741.5'973--dc20   95-11360
                                                       CIP

TABLE OF CONTENTS

This book is dedicated with love to
Tom, Isaac and Amy

GARDEN VARIETY GUYS

There's a commercial where guys sit around drinking beer, cleaning fish, wiping their noses on their sleeves and saying, "It doesn't get any better than this." That's not a commercial. That's a warning.

—Diane Jordan

GUYS

ARE DIFFERENT
THAN

OTHER HUMANS.

Philip:

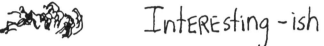

Interesting - ish

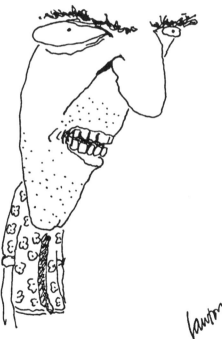

lawtn

"Hi! I'M ONE OF THOSE LOUDER-THAN-EVERYONE-ELSE-IN-PUBLIC-AND-OBLIVIOUS-TO-IT TYPES."

CHAS. :

Much more
interesting
in memory
than in
Actual life.

Lawton

HANK:

Uses nasal noises
to
"break the ice."

SSSSNNNOORT!!!

lawton

LLOYD:

A MAN WHO WOULDN'T KNOW A GOOD TIME IF IT HIT HIM ON THE HEAD, KNOCKED HIM OUT COLD, TIED HIS HANDS AND FEET, AND LEFT HIM IN A LITTLE TOOL SHED TO PERISH.

R. Chast

The Traditional Male

"Macho does not prove mucho."
—Zsa Zsa Gabor

HOW ANIMALS MARK THEIR TERRITORY.

THE PARTY ANIMAL

"Men are the speed bumps on the highway of life."

—bumper sticker

A dreaded 'Clone' style Hetero-Swinger!

CONT.

WHITE BOY WITH THE BEET

A
MAN'S BEST FRIEND

When I was in third grade, there was
a kid running for office. His slogan
was: 'Vote for me and I'll show you my
wee-wee.' He won by a landslide.
—Dorothy, "The Golden Girls"

OFFROAD ADVENTURES

**How many roads must a man travel
down before he admits he is lost?**
—T-shirt slogan

Two ways to tell if a man has a small penis:

ACTUAL EXTENT OF DOUG'S OFF-ROAD ADVENTURES.
(SEE BOX FOR DETAIL)

THE MALE MIND

Men can read maps better than women. 'Cause only the male mind could conceive of one inch equaling a hundred miles.

—Roseanne Arnold

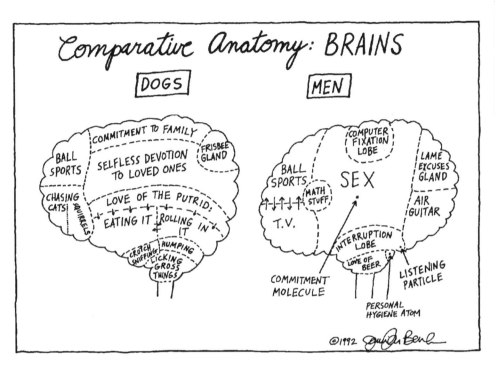

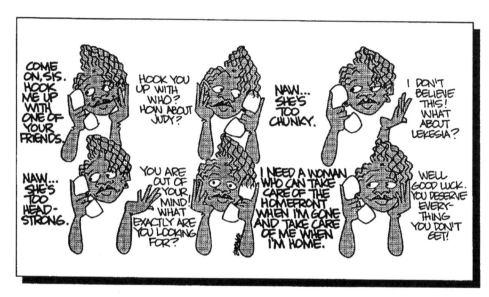

MALE PATTERN BLINDNESS

I WOULDN'T **REALLY** DO THIS — I DON'T HAVE A CAR!

LOST GUYS

Q: If a man and a woman jumped off
a 10-story building at the same
time, which one would land first?

A: The woman. The man would get
lost.

THE ISLAND OF LOST GUYS
I was in a gigantic shopping mall in Flagstaff, Arizona!
I was driving to my sister-in-law's on a series of teeny-weeny dirt roads!
I was trying to get to Shea Stadium, but they made us keep switching trains!
R. Chast

Impossible Men

If they can put one man on the moon why can't
they put them all there?

—Chocolate Waters

"I take it back. You are in touch with your emotions! You certainly know Anger, irritation and hostility intimately"

-DON'T YOU THINK IT'S A BIT *MEAN*?

IT'S A *COMIC*, JAKE! I'M *NOT* DR.-FUCKING-*RUTH*!!!

WHAT DO *YOU*?? WANT?

Confused? Now's the time to
Ask Aunt Violet

Q: I'm a slow eater, one of the slowest in history. When I go to restaurants with my boyfriend, he shovels it in within 10 minutes, then shoots me daggers while drumming his fingers on the table for the next 15. Help!! —Laura C.

A: THE PROBLEM IS *NOT* THAT YOU'RE A *SLOW EATER*; THE PROBLEM IS THAT YOUR *BOYFRIEND IS A RUDE, SELFISH* LOUT.

HE REMINDS ME OF THOSE *WISE-GUYS* IN JUNIOR HIGH WHO USED TO WAD UP *TOILET PAPER* AND FLING IT ON THE ACOUSTICAL CEILING.

DON'T YOU TWO *TALK* OVER DINNER? WHAT HAPPENED TO THE ANCIENT ART OF CONVERSATION?

WRONG
RIGHT

I'M SORRY I'M EATING SO SLOWLY. I'M *SUCH* AN IDIOT. GRUNT

CHOMSKY SAYS THAT SYNTACTIC ABILITY IS *BIOLOGICALLY* DETERMINED... I LOVE YOUR MIND

HIS PROBLEM IS PROBABLY DUE TO *POOR EATING HABITS* LEARNED AS A CHILD.

HOWEVER, IF THIS *BOORISH* BEHAVIOR KEEPS UP, FORGET HIM. JERKS LIKE *THAT* DON'T MAKE THE GREATEST *SEX PARTNERS*, EITHER.

OH DONALD I'M SORRY I'M SUCH AN IDIOT... GRUNT.

©1993 C.Leschen

"I don't know, but whenever I come in here, I start to feel nostalgic for Vinnie..."

GAY MEN

This guy says, "I'm perfect for you, 'cause I'm a cross between a macho and a sensitive man." I said, "Oh, a gay trucker?"

—Judy Tenuta

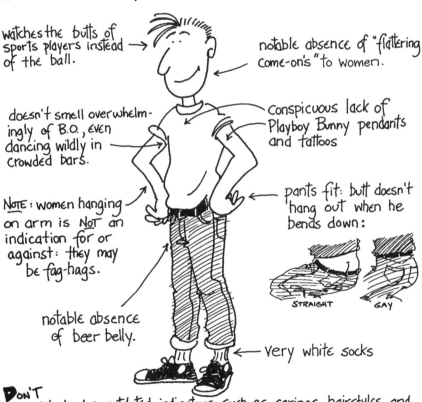

SPOT THOSE GAY GUYS!!

FAG HAGS!... don't waste your time on sensitive straight men!
STRAIGHT WOMEN!... looking to become a fag-hag?
GAY MEN!... are you giving out the wrong signals to Mr. Right?
HET GUYS... need a buddy who won't hit on "your woman"?

Watches the butts of sports players instead of the ball.

notable absence of "flattering come-on's" to women.

doesn't smell overwhelmingly of B.O., even dancing wildly in crowded bars.

Conspicuous lack of Playboy Bunny pendants and tattoos

NOTE: women hanging on arm is NOT an indication for or against: they may be fag-hags.

pants fit: butt doesn't hang out when he bends down:

STRAIGHT   GAY

notable absence of beer belly.

very white socks

DON'T be misled by outdated indicators such as earings, hairstyles and artsy-fartsy professions... beware of straight "gay chic".

©1993 leanne franson

CITY of COMRADES IN ARMS LOVE.™

THOSE FOLKS WHO OPPOSE GAYS IN THE MILITARY... YOU KNOW, THEY'VE GOT *A POINT*. AFTER ALL, EVERYONE KNOWS THE ARMED FORCES ARE AN *ABSOLUTE BREEDING GROUND* FOR CLASS A *ROMANTIC ADVENTURE*. JUST CONSIDER...

THE *FLAMBOYANCE* AND *SPONTANEITY*...

HUBBA HUBBA, SIR!

THE *CLOSE QUARTERS*...

IT'S 140 DEGREES IN HERE, *PITCH DARK* AND FULL OF *AMMO* BUT I'M STARTIN' TO GET A LITTLE *ITCH!*

THE *GLAMOUR*...

MAN! THIS IS GETTING ME *HOT* LIKE YOU WOULDN'T *BELIEVE!*

NOT TO MENTION THE MOST SEDUCTIVE THING OF *ALL*: THE *UNLIMITED OPPORTUNITIES* FOR FURTIVE *ROMANTIC LIAISONS*...

AS SOON AS I FIGURE OUT HOW TO *BREATHE* IN THIS THING, I'M GONNA GET ME SOME *ACTION!*

© 1993 K. BROWN

BILL AND BRIAN'S DREAMHOUSE

 Dating Men

I'm dating the Pope. Actually I'm just using him to get to God.

—Judy Tenuta

STORY MINUTE © 1993
ZENO'S PARADOX CAROL LAY

AFTER THEIR FIRST DATE HE KISSED HER TWICE AND GAVE HER A HUG.

ON THEIR SECOND DATE, SHE GOT ONE LITTLE PECK ON THE CHEEK.

ON THEIR THIRD DATE, HE SHOOK HER HAND POLITELY AND LEFT.

ON THEIR FOURTH DATE, HE JUST SAID GOODNIGHT AT THE DOOR.

ON THEIR FIFTH DATE, HE WAVED GOODBYE FROM ACROSS THE STREET.

ON THEIR SIXTH DATE, HE HIRED SOMEONE TO SAY GOODNIGHT FOR HIM.

Uh....GOODNIGHT.

ON THEIR SEVENTH DATE, HE MOVED OUT OF TOWN AND LEFT NO FORWARDING ADDRESS.

BUT, LOOKING BACK, SHE HAD TO ADMIT THAT HE'D BEEN THE PERFECT GENTLEMAN.

Sigh

STRIP TIS by Stephanie

" of course my ex is going out
with someone much younger...
Someone his own age would see
right through him!"

WOMEN TRADING PICK-UP LINES

CONT.

CONT.

Story Minute © 1992
"WE EAT INSOMNIACS" CAROL LAY

TONIGHT SHE WOULD AUDITION THIS GUY FOR THE ROLE OF "NEW BOYFRIEND."

SO FAR, SO GOOD. HE HAD STYLE, TALENT, AND YOUTHFUL ENERGY.

IT WASN'T SEX THAT MATTERED SO MUCH AS WHETHER THEY COULD ACTUALLY SLEEP WELL TOGETHER.

UNFORTUNATELY, THE SAME YOUTHFUL ENERGY THAT MADE HIM A GOOD LOVER MADE HIM TOSS AND TURN ALL NIGHT.

NO SOONER WOULD SHE START TO DREAM WHEN REALITY WOULD SMACK HER IN THE FACE.

FINALLY, HE STAYED STILL LONG ENOUGH FOR HER TO START DOZING.

ZZZ

HEY! YOU'RE SNORING!

BUT THEN...

IT WILL PROBABLY BE SEVERAL MONTHS BEFORE AUDITIONS START UP AGAIN.

MEN & SEX

If men really knew how to do it, they wouldn't
have to pay for it.

—Roseanne Arnold

WORKING MEN

I have yet to hear a man ask for advice on how to combine marriage and a career.

—Gloria Steinem

THE BIRTH OF STANLEY MARTIN, C.P.A.

MARRIED MEN

A man in love is incomplete until he's married—
then he's finished.

—Zsa Zsa Gabor

SHUT UP! Jesus, didn't you people get to VOTE on TUESDAY?

OH NO!

RAT-OY!

DO IT!

WHAT DO YOU?? WANT

HEY!

Confused? Now's the time to
Ask Aunt Violet

Q: My husband only wants to see the crappiest movies. He's always getting excited about the latest *Steven Spielberg* or *Star Trek* extravaganza. The other day he even rented *Terminator II!* He never wants to see anything intelligent or insightful like he used to. I'm starting to think I should've married someone else. What do *you* think?   —Film Fatale

A: YES, YOU SHOULD'VE MARRIED SOMEONE ELSE, BUT, ALAS, YOU DIDN'T. I SENSE HE'S JUST ROOTING FOR ALL THIS VIOLENT, SEXIST, RACIST, OBTUSE JUNK AS A WAY TO *ASSERT HIS MASCULINITY.*

LET 'IM! GIVE THE GUY SOME *SPACE.* YOU DO HAVE OTHER OPTIONS.

FOR ONE, WHILE HE'S OUT SEEING *"MORONS FROM OUTER SPACE",* YOU CAN GO SEE *"TWO AVERAGE GIRLS ON AN AVERAGE DAY WHEN NOTHING HAPPENS IN A DREARY, MID-SIZED INDUSTRIAL NORTHERN ENGLISH TOWN",* WHICH I HEAR IS PRETTY GOOD...

EXCUSE ME, WOULD YOU MIND MOVING OVER SO MY *ARTSY, INTELLECTUAL BOYFRIEND* WHO *LOVES* THESE KINDS OF FILMS CAN SIT THERE? WE WANT TO *MAKE OUT* THROUGH THE WHOLE SHOW..

MILKY STUDS

OR YOU *CAN* GO OUT WITH *OTHER* FRIENDS, YOU KNOW.

I WANNA SEE "THE HOUSE, THE AUDIENCE AND THE REALLY BIG ADMISSION FEE"

THAT SOUNDS DROLL. WHAT A-BOUT THIS MIKE LEIGH FESTIVAL AT THE PACIFIC FILM ARCHIVE?

IF BY *THIS* TIME HE DOESN'T START CRAVING EITHER YOUR *COMPANY* OR A LITTLE *CEREBRAL* STIMULATION, FUCK 'IM. JOIN THE *FILM SOCIETY* AND HAVE AN AFFAIR...

GOD HE LOOKS JUST LIKE FRANK LANGELLA IN "DIARY OF A MAD HOUSEWIFE"

OH YES!

I NOTICE YOU'RE READING "THE FRENCH NEW WAVE AS A SEXIST, FASCIST MANIFESTO" BY SUSAN SON-TAG-SOAM!

WHO KNOWS, AFTER AWHILE YOU MAY ACTUALLY START *MISSING* YOUR *HUSBAND.*

OK-SO IT'S EITHER THE JOHN CAGE BIOGRAPHY OR "A GODDARDIAN LOOK AT JAPANESE DOCUMENTARY CINEMA".

HOW ABOUT "WAYNE'S WORLD"?

MOVIE

©1992 11/3 CARYN LESCHEN

MEN AND HOUSEWORK

"If a man's home is his castle...let him clean it."
—bumper sticker

ANTi-SEXiST MEN DO
THE HOOVERING —

FATHERS

Before accepting a marriage proposal, take a good look at his father. If he's still handsome, witty, and has all his teeth...marry him instead.

—Diane Jordan

"I just felt like I wasn't spending enough time
with the kids."

"I JUST WANT YOU TO KNOW,   "THANKS, DAD."
YOU'RE LIKE A SON TO ME."

TALKING TO GUYS

My grandmother's 90. She's dating. He's 93. It's going great. They never argue. They can't hear each other.

—Cathy Ladman

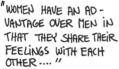

"WOMEN HAVE AN AD-VANTAGE OVER MEN IN THAT THEY SHARE THEIR FEELINGS WITH EACH OTHER...."

"MEN NEED TO DEVELOP THEIR OWN WAYS OF CONFIDING IN EACH OTHER AND COMMUNICATING THEIR INNER FEELINGS IN AN ATMOSPHERE OF MUTUAL SUPPORT...."

UM, JERRY?... DO YOU EVER FEEL ...WELL.... LIKE YOU'RE JUST NOT GOOD ENOUGH?...LIKE NO MATTER WHAT YOU DO, YOU'LL NEVER MEASURE UP TO SOCIETY'S EXPECTATIONS OF A MAN?

© SUDDICK 91

SO... YOU THINK THE 49ERS ARE GONNA GET IT TOGETHER OR WHAT?

PERFECT MEN

A good man doesn't just happen. They have to be created by us women. A guy is a lump like a doughnut. So, first you gotta get rid of all the stuff his mom did to him, and then you gotta get rid of all that macho crap that they pick up from the beer commercials. And then there's my personal favorite, the male ego.

—Roseanne Arnold

"I'd like to find a man who's sensitive
in general, and macho in emergencies."

FANTASY MEN

I want a man who's kind and understanding. Is that too much to ask of a millionaire?

—Zsa Zsa Gabor

"This is Harry. He doesn't exist...
he's just a fantasy I have from
time to time..."

"Why settle for dwarves...?"
she asked herself...

Story Minute ©1993 CAROL LAY
"FAUST LOVE"
THE SCULPTRESS WAS LONELY AND INTENSELY DISSATISFIED...
COLD... COLD...

PRETTY MUCH LIKE **REAL MEN**, I MUST SAY...

I'D SELL MY SOUL FOR A MAN WITH THE STUFF THAT COULD SET A FIRE IN **MY** HEART...

...IF I COULD BE SURE I **HAD** A SOUL, THAT IS.
SOMETIMES I WONDER...
OF **COURSE** YOU HAVE A SOUL!

--AND IF YOU SIGN IT OVER TO **ME** YOU CAN HAVE THE LOVE OF **ANY MAN** YOU WANT.

ANY MAN?
YES, ANY MAN AT ALL.

CONT.

Mirabelle Guiles, Detective to the STARS...

★ ★ ★ AND the CASE of the "FAUX FABIOS"

©1993 BY NICOLE HOLLANDER

RITA, COULD you BRING ME A PLATE OF MACADAMIA NUTS AND SOME COLESLAW?

I WAS ADMIRING MY NEW LetterHEAD, "Mirabelle Guiles, Detective to STARS of NO PARTICULAR TALENT," WHEN I LOOKED UP INTO the eyes of the MAN WITH ONE NAME. MY KNEES TREMBLED. "CAN I HELP YOU?" I ASKED, STUTTERING SLIGHTLY. "Someone's been STEALING MY USED RAZORS," HE SAID, GENTLY touching HiS trade-MARKED SHAVED CHEST. "OH, Let me Do THAT "I SAID, FALLING over the desk AND DISCHARGING MY GUN iNTO the CEILING.

Nicole Hollander

EPILOGUE

Q: Can you imagine a world without men?

A: No crime, and lots of happy fat women.

—Nicole Hollander

About the Editor

Roz Warren is the editor of the ground-breaking Women's Glib humor collection. She is a happily married radical feminist mom, grew up in Detroit, graduated from the University of Chicago and received her law degree from Boston University Law School. Roz practiced law until the birth of her son, seven years ago. Now an at-home mom, she spends Quantity Time with son Thomas.

Other humor books by
Roz Warren

Women's Glib: A Collection of Women's Humor
Women's Glibber: State-of-the-Art Women's Humor
Glibquips: Funny Words by Funny Women
What Is This Thing Called Sex?: Cartoons by Women
The Best Contemporary Women's Humor Collection